MW01274663

It's Elemental

Lessons that Engage

Don Dupont

and

Brian Hiller

ISBN 978-0-934017-55-8

Michael D. Bennett, editor

Memphis Musicraft Publications
4096 Blue Cedar, Lakeland, TN 38002

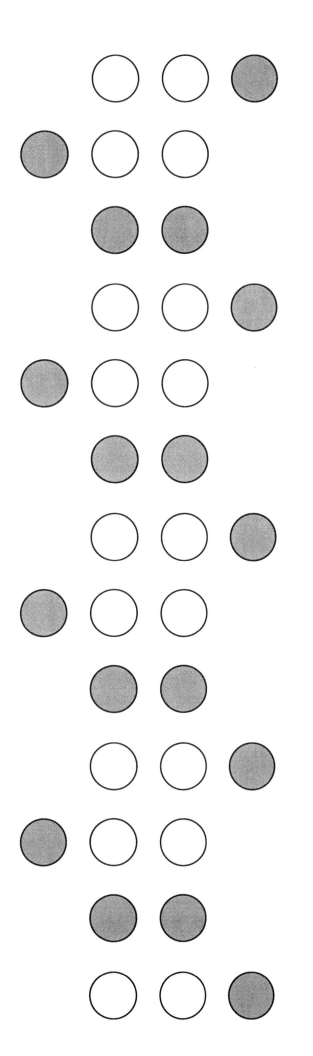

Contents

© 2002, **Memphis Musicraft Publications**

All rights reserved. No part of this publication may be reproduced or distributed in any form without the expressed permission of the publisher. Exception: The visuals in the lessons may be reproduced for single classroom use.

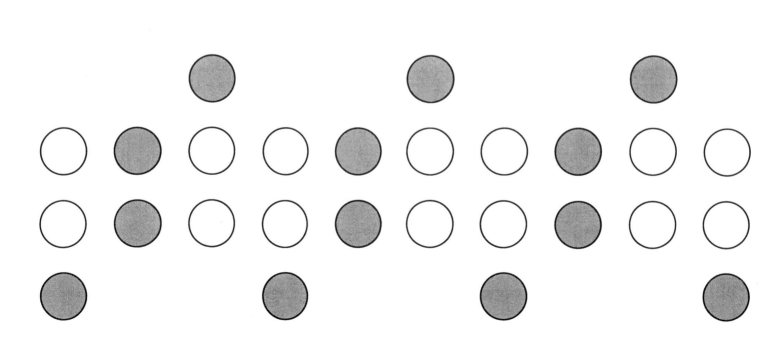

Preface

It's Elemental: Lessons that Engage is a collection of fifteen fully-processed lessons intended to enhance the curricular goals of your elementary music classroom. The material presented contains traditional, folk and original songs and poems as well as orchestrations, movement and game suggestions. The lessons integrate the elements of Orff Schulwerk through singing, speech, movement and instrument playing.

The collection is organized into five sections: **Rhythm, Melody, Form, Texture** and **Harmony.** Each section includes three lessons, one each for early, middle and upper elementary students. The grade levels suggested are meant to be guides. The experience and level of your students will determine the grade at which each lesson is presented.

Focus: Each lesson is geared toward a specific focus, an emphasis on a particular musical concept.

Skills: The skills listed at the beginning of the lessons are the prior knowledge and abilities students need in order to successfully complete each lesson.

Process: The process begins with an activity that engages the learner, reviews concepts, and supports the focus. The steps that follow are carefully designed to lead the students toward the desired outcome.

Performance: The lesson culminates in a performance. Here the students demonstrate understanding of the focus.

Extension: Each lesson includes an extension, which can be used to further enhance the learning.

Classroom Tip: Finally, a classroom tip provides little tidbits about classroom management, organization and routines.

The orchestrations in the collection are prepared using body percussion and text phrases. The body percussion is demonstrated by the teacher, mirrored by the students, then transferred to the instruments. Text phrases help students play their parts more accurately. Once parts are learned, the text phrases are internalized. We have kept the orchestrations simple so they can be learned quickly and easily. Feel free to adjust them to meet the needs and abilities of your students.

Although we have provided a step-by-step process, we encourage you to make these lessons your own by using your strengths and talents and those of your students. We hope you enjoy the collection and wish you much success.

We are grateful to Carol Huffman, Donna Basile and Robert de Frece for their generous support, guidance and friendship. We also wish to thank our editor for his vision and dedication to this project. Finally, we dedicate this book to our family and dear friends for their support and patience during this process!

Don Dupont
Brian Hiller

Focus On Rhythm

This Little Song

Dupont

This lit-tle song is not ve-ry long, just lis-ten well and fol-low a - long.

Coda

1. Touch your head. x x x x x x
2. Clap your hands.
3. Pat your legs.
4. Stamp your feet.

This lit-tle song was

not ve-ry long. We lis-tened well and fol-lowed a - long. Hoo - ray!

This Little Song
(Extended Version)

Dupont

This lit-tle song is not ve-ry long, just lis-ten well and fol-low a - long. Touch your

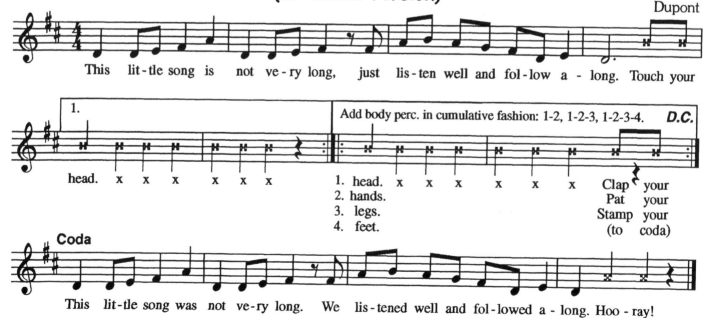

1.

head. x x x x x x

Add body perc. in cumulative fashion: 1-2, 1-2-3, 1-2-3-4. **D.C.**

1. head. x x x x x x
2. hands.
3. legs.
4. feet.

Clap your
Pat your
Stamp your
(to coda)

Coda

This lit-tle song was not ve-ry long. We lis-tened well and fol-lowed a - long. Hoo - ray!

This Little Song

FOCUS: Steady beat

SKILLS: Body percussion • Unpitched instrument playing

PROCESS

☼   Perform body percussion/body movements to a steady beat as students imitate simultaneously. Change movements every eight beats. Outline the body percussion used in the song. Suggested music: Mozart's *Eine Kleine Nachtmusik*, first movement.

☼   Sing *This Little Song*, performing body percussion as indicated. Students imitate simultaneously.

☼   Teach the song, echoing by phrases. Perform using body percussion.

☼   Teach the Coda, adding a gesture on "Hooray!"

PERFORMANCE

Song with body percussion

EXTENSION 1 - Unpitched instrument playing

Transfer the body percussion to unpitched percussion. For example:

> *Touch your head.   =   Shake your bells.*
> *Clap your hands.   =   Click your sticks.*
> *Pat your legs.   =   Tap your block.*
> *Stamp your feet.   =   Play your drum.*

Divide class into four groups, one group for each instrument. Sing the song and have each group play its instrument when named.

EXTENSION 2 - Cumulative singing

Using the extended version of the song, perform the body percussion section in cumulative fashion as indicated.

Transfer to unpitched percussion as shown in Extension 1 for an additional challenge.

CLASSROOM TIP — Self Space

For activities such as this we have students stand in their bubble space (self space). To find their bubble space students spread out in the room. They stand with arms outstretched and slowly turn in place, making sure not to touch anyone or anything nearby. Once they can do this, they blow an imaginary bubble around themselves. Students then practice moving around in their self space taking care not to let their bubbles pop!

One Bottle O' Pop

Verse 1

One bot-tle o' pop, two bot-tle o' pop, three bot-tle o' pop, four bot-tle o' pop,

five bot-tle o' pop, six bot-tle o' pop, se-ven bot-tle o' pop. Pop!

Verse 2

Don't throw your junk in my back yard, my back yard, my back yard.

Don't throw your junk in my back yard, my back yard's full!

Verse 3

Fish and chips and vin-e-gar, vin-e-gar, vin-e-gar,

Fish and chips and vin-e-gar, pep-per, pep-per, pep-per, salt!

One Bottle O' Pop

FOCUS: Triple meter

LEVEL: 3 - 4

SKILLS: Three-part singing • Duple meter • Movement

PROCESS

☼ In pairs, have students perform the two-beat pattern while speaking the text. Once students are secure, perform the three-beat pattern in similar fashion.

pat legs | clap own hands | pat legs | clap own hands | pat partner's hands

Ap - ple | *Straw - ber - ry*

✿ Lead students in performing combinations of the duple and triple meter patterns. Using a drum and mallet, tap the center of the drum on "one" and the rim on the weak beats. Play combinations of the patterns as students speak and perform them. At first say "two" or "three" to announce the meter at the beginning of each change. Then have students perform the changes without prompts.

✿ Sing *One Bottle O' Pop*. Then teach each verse, echoing by phrases. Once familiar with the song, students may sing it while performing the three-beat pattern with partners.

✿ Movement: Divide into three groups—one group for each verse. Step to the dotted half note pulse.
Verse 1 formation: One straight line, students count off by 1's and 2's.
  Meas. 1: Step (1's fwd., 2's bwd.)
  Meas. 2: Together
  Meas. 3: Step (1's bwd., 2's fwd.)
  Meas. 4: Together
  Meas. 5-8: Repeat measures 1-4

Verse 2 formation: Circle in place, students in pairs. Establish "partner" and "neighbor."
  Meas. 1: (Face partner for meas. 1-4.) Wag fingers at each other
  Meas. 2: Glare at partner with hands on hips
  Meas. 3-4: Repeat
  Meas. 5-8: (Face neighbor for meas. 5-8) Repeat motions from measures 1-4

Verse 3 formation: Pairs, one behind the other, hands on hips.
  Meas. 1: Front student leans L, rear student leans R
  Meas. 2: Return to beginning positions
  Meas. 3: Front student leans R, rear student leans L
  Meas. 4: Return to beginning positions
  Meas. 5-8: Repeat

PERFORMANCE

Song without movement
Groups sing their verses with movement
Layer in each verse of the song until all are singing

EXTENSION - Read and write in triple meter

To further reinforce triple meter we like to use rhythmic exercises such as the one below. Students perform the rhythms first with body percussion, then transfer to unpitched percussion and finally to barred instrument improvisation. When students are secure, we encourage them to compose their own triple meter rhythm pieces.

CLASSROOM TIP - Meter Ball Bounce

Our students enjoy using a tennis ball to further explore meter. Standing in pairs, the students perform the following pattern: For duple meter—"bounce, catch, bounce, catch." For triple meter—"bounce, catch, hold, bounce, catch, hold." We do this to recorded music in duple and triple meter.

Chicken on the Fence Post

Traditional
arr. Hiller

Chicken on the Fence Post

FOCUS: Sixteenth notes

SKILLS: Moving bordun • Folk dance • Barred instrument playing

PROCESS

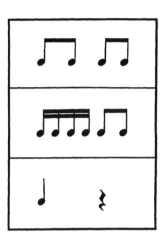

☼ Review the two-beat rhythm patterns using a visual. Speak and clap rhythm syllables as students echo. Repeat, outlining the rhythm of the song.

☼ Teach *Chicken on the Fence Post*, echoing by phrases. Have students indicate where sixteenth note rhythms occur.

☼ Prepare the orchestration with body percussion and text phrases, then transfer to instruments.

☼ Folk Dance: Formation—concentric circles, partners facing each other, one in each circle. Students step R, circles move in opposite directions.
Meas. 1: Side - close (new partner)
Meas. 2: Pat own legs, clap own hands (in place)
Meas. 3-4: Repeat measures 1 and 2
Meas. 5-6: Repeat measures 1 and 2
Meas. 7-8: Pat own legs, clap own hands, pat partner's hands (in place)

☼ Teach the interlude, echoing by phrases.

PERFORMANCE

Intro
Song with dance
Interlude: Students bounce to the beat, hands on knees, and wave good-bye to partner on "gone to town."
Song with dance

EXTENSION - Rhymin' Josie

Students will enjoy creating new conclusions for the interlude. For example:
. . . *Can't dance with me 'cause she's got a frown.*
. . . *Can't dance with me 'cause she's upside down.*

CLASSROOM TIP — Class List

In order for students to have an equal number of turns at the instruments we use a class list. We invite students to play in the order they appear on the list and place a check next to their names. At the next lesson we begin from where we left off. This deters students from clamoring for a particular instrument and avoids a common error— assigning instruments to the best players!

Focus On Melody

Teddy Bear

Swing ♩♪ = ⌐3⌐ ♩ ♪

American Play Song

Ted - dy Bear, Ted - dy Bear, turn a - round,_____
Ted - dy Bear, Ted - dy Bear, turn climb the stairs,_____

Ted - dy Bear, Ted - dy Bear, touch the ground.
Ted - dy Bear, Ted - dy Bear, say your prayers.

Ted - dy Bear, Ted - dy Bear, show your shoe,_____
Ted - dy Bear, Ted - dy Bear, turn off the light,_____

Ted - dy Bear, Ted - dy Bear, that will do.
Ted - dy Bear, Ted - dy Bear, say, "Good night."

SO   SO   SO   SO

mi ———   mi ———

Teddy Bear

FOCUS: *So - Mi*

SKILLS: High-low • Barred instrument playing

PROCESS

☆ With students in self space, explore ways of moving high and low. Play high and low phrases on a piano or bass xylophone to lead the students' movements.

☆ Sing *Teddy Bear*, performing motions described in the text. Have students simultaneously imitate the motions.

☆ Teach the song, echoing by phrases. Once students are familiar with the song, have them sing it with motions. Then isolate the *so - mi* motives by touching heads on "Ted-dy" and shoulders on "Bear."

☆ Display the *Teddy Bear* visual. As students sing, point to the bears in rhythm each time "Ted-dy Bear" is sung.

PERFORMANCE

Song with motions
Song with motions, but sing "Ted-dy Bear" motives only. Internalize all other text while performing the motions.

TEDDY BEAR GAME - Circle formation

Sing each student's name twice using *so - mi* motives; students echo. Maintain a steady drum beat.

Next, have class sing *Teddy Bear*, substituting students' names in place of each "Ted-dy Bear" motive. The named student acts out the movement after his/her name. Continue until all have had a turn.

EXTENSION - Barred instrument playing

Remove all bars except G and E. Have students practice playing the "Ted-dy Bear" motive. Sing the song substituting instruments for "Ted-dy Bear."

For further practice singing *so - mi* motives, create additional verses to the song using rhyming words. Examples:
Teddy Bear, Teddy Bear wear your hat, Teddy Bear, Teddy Bear, swing your bat.
Teddy Bear, Teddy Bear shut the gate, Teddy Bear, Teddy Bear don't be late.

CLASSROOM TIP — In-Tune Teddy

As a warm-up we use a Teddy Bear hand puppet to foster in-tune singing. Students echo motives used in the song, first on "loo" then with solfege—so-mi, so-so-mi, so-la-so, so-la-so-mi. The puppet does a brief dance when the singing is in-tune. Keep the patterns moving smoothly.

Rocky Mountain

American Folk Song
arr. Dupont/Hiller

Rocky Mountain

FOCUS: *Do, Re, Mi, So, La*

SKILLS: Solfege/hand signs • Instrument playing • Movement

| LA |
| SO |
| |
| MI |
| RE |
| DO |

PROCESS

☆ Review *Do, Re, Mi, So, La* using solfege syllables and hand signs. Echo short motives that include steps and skips.

☆ Teach *Rocky Mountain* as follows:
Sing the song for the class using the solfege pitch ladder. Point out steps and skips.
Teach the song, echoing by phrases using solfege and hand signs.
Teach the song with lyrics, echoing by phrases using hand signs.

☆ Prepare the orchestration with body percussion and text phrases, then transfer to instruments.

☆ Movement: Form an alley of partners. (Clap = clap own hands. Pat = pat partner's hands.)
Meas. 1-2: Step (fwd) - together - clap - pat
Meas. 3-4: Step (bwd) - together - clap - clap
Meas. 5-8: Repeat
Meas. 9-12: Head couple slides down the alley while all *side-close* 4x in opposite direction.
Meas. 13-16: All *do-si-do* partners

☆ Teach the interlude, echoing by phrases.

PERFORMANCE

Intro: BX/BM, four measures
Song with orchestration/dance
Interlude
Song with orchestration/dance

EXTENSION   *MI - RE - DO* Game

Preparation: With students seated at barred instruments, remove all bars except F-G-A-C-D. Sing three-pitch phrases using solfege; students echo. Next, sing the same phrases using letter names; students echo. Sing the phrases again with solfege as students transfer to barred instruments. Have students identify the bars which correspond to *Do - Re - Mi - So - La*.

The Game: Sing three-pitch phrases using solfege. Have students echo the phrases on barred instruments **except for *Mi-Re-Do* patterns**. If any students play *Mi-Re-Do* patterns, teacher earns a point. If no one plays, the class earns a point.

CLASSROOM TIP - Movement Process

We teach our students to internalize the movement vocabulary for each dance. First they speak the movement in rhythm, then speak and perform the movement, finally perform it without speaking. This takes a little extra time at first but saves a lot of correcting time later.

America, America

America, America

FOCUS: Aeolian (natural minor) mode

SKILLS: Instrument/recorder playing • Crossover bordun • Movement

PROCESS

☆ Display a major scale pitch ladder. Sing *Hot Cross Buns* in G Major using solfege and hand signs, echoing by phrases. Identify *"Do"* as the tonal center.

☆ Display a minor scale pitch ladder. Sing *Hot Cross Buns* in E Minor using solfege and hand signs. Identify *"La"* as the tonal center. Have students describe the difference between the two versions.

☆ Have sudents play both versions of *Hot Cross Buns* on barred instruments. Add F# (ti) for the minor version. Add bordun accompaniment if desired.

☆ Teach *America, America*, echoing by phrases.

☆ Teach the soprano recorder (SR) part, echoing by phrases.

☆ Prepare the orchestration with body percussion and text phrases, then transfer to instruments.

☆ Movement: Groups of four students in circle formation, hands joined.
Meas. 1: Step (in) - touch - (raise arms slowly)
Meas. 2: Step (out) - touch - (lower arms slowly)
Meas. 3-4: Repeat
Meas. 5-6: Step - 2 - 3 - together (One pair of opposite partners touches outstretched palms and changes places.)
Meas. 7-8: Other pair repeats

DO	
TI	
LA	LA
SO	SO
FA	FA
MI	MI
RE	RE
DO	DO
	TI
	LA

PERFORMANCE

Intro: BX/BM, SM/AM, 2 measures
Verse 1: Song/dance with orchestration (no recorder)
Verse 2: Song/dance with orchestration plus recorder

EXTENSION - Create Cinquains

Students work in groups to create cinquain poetry describing the beauty of America. Have students add sound color (tone clusters, glissandos, tremolos) and movement to enhance their creations. These verses can be used with *America, America* to create a rondo.

A cinquain is usually a twenty-two syllable, five-line poem:
1st line: two syllables   2nd line: four syllables
3rd line: six syllables   4th line: eight syllables
5th line: two syllables

Example
Mountains
Rise up touching
The vast and sunset sky
As colors of gold and purple
Entwine

CLASSROOM TIP - Legato Style

Encourage good vocal production and interpretation by having students sing in legato style that gradually gets louder, then softer at the end. We have our students visualize "gliding on the ice" to produce a smooth sound. They slowly stretch out their arms during the first half of the song then bring them back during the second half to represent this change in dynamics.

Focus On Form

Hear the Train

Dupont/Hiller

Hear the Train

FOCUS: Binary (A-B) form

LEVEL: K-1

SKILLS: Steady beat • Rhythmic speech • Instrument playing

PROCESS

☺ Teach students the following train sound rhythms. Have students practice the sounds, then choose their two favorites. Divide class in half, one group for each sound. Create contrasting movement to accompany the sounds. Perform in two sections—A then B.

choo - choo, choo-choo   chug - ga, chug - ga, chug - ga, chug - ga   Toot! Toot!

☺ Teach the A section of *Hear the Train*, echoing by phrases.

☺ Prepare the orchestration with body percussion and text phrases, then transfer to instruments.

☺ Teach the B section, echoing by phrases.

☺ <u>Train Game:</u> Form one circle with a student (conductor) in the center.
During the A section the conductor maintains a steady beat on his/her legs as others mirror. On the repeat the conductor uses a different body percussion, which is mirrored by the group.

During the B section students in the circle walk the beat CCW while moving their arms like the wheels of a train. On "toot" all stop and "pull the whistle rope" with their outside hands.

Teach the Interlude, echoing by phrases. Insert a new student's name as indicated. He/she goes into the center of the circle and becomes the new conductor as the game continues. Play until all students have had a turn.

PERFORMANCE

A: Song with orchestration
B: Speech with movement
Interlude

Repeat as needed.

EXTENSION - Let's Move!

With students in pairs, teach two contrasting movements (ex: join hands and sway - lock arms and walk in a circle). Play the beat on a drum for one movement and on a suspended cymbal for the other. Have students listen and change movements as the instruments change.

Play *Minuet in G* by J. S. Bach. Have students perform one movement during the A section and the other during the B section.

CLASSROOM TIP — Student Conductors

We often use student conductors when someone is having trouble playing his/her part with rhythmic accuracy. The conductor sits in front of the student and mirrors the playing of the instrument with the student. A second benefit: additional students get an opportunity to practice "playing" the instrument parts.

Georgie Porgie

Nursery Rhyme
arr. Dupont/Hiller

B Verse 1
Pudding and pie, pudding and pie,
Georgie Porgie made me cry!
Pudding and pie, pudding and pie,
If he comes back I think I'll die!

Movement (Circle Formation)
step (in) - 2 - 3 - together
hands on cheeks
step (out) - 2 - 3 - together
shake finger 4 times

C Verse 2
Peaches and cream, peaches and cream,
Georgie Porgie made a scene!
Peaches and cream, peaches and cream,
If he comes back I think I'll scream!

sidestep R - close - sidestep - close
hands to sides of mouth
sidestep L - close - sidestep - close
fold arms, bounce to the beat

D Verse 3
Cookies and cake, cookies and cake,
Georgie Porgie made me shake!
Cookies and cake, cookies and cake,
Please come back for goodness sake!

do-si-do partner
reach hands high, shaking them
do-si-do corner
clasp hands, pleading

Georgie Porgie

FOCUS: Rondo form

SKILLS: Rhythmic speech • 6/8 meter • Movement • Instrument playing

PROCESS

☺ *Teach Dessert Rondo,* echoing by phrases. Divide class into three groups for B, C, and D. Have all students speak A. Perform in rondo form: A B A C A D A. Encourage expressive rhythmic speech.

Dessert Rondo

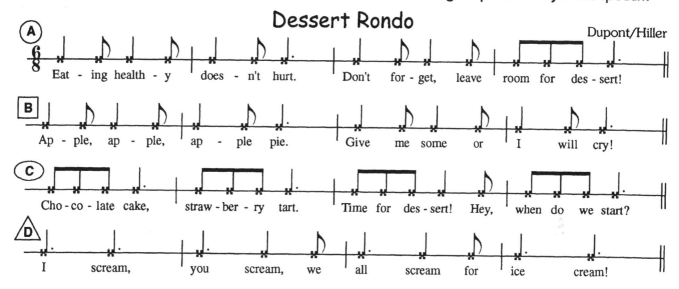

Dupont/Hiller

A: Eat - ing health - y does - n't hurt. Don't for - get, leave room for des - sert!

B: Ap - ple, ap - ple, ap - ple pie. Give me some or I will cry!

C: Cho - co - late cake, straw - ber - ry tart. Time for des - sert! Hey, when do we start?

D: I scream, you scream, we all scream for ice cream!

☹ Teach *Georgie Porgie,* echoing by phrases.

☺ Prepare the orchestration with body percussion and text phrases, then transfer to instruments.

☺ <u>A Section Movement:</u> Form three groups in circle formation.
   Meas. 1-2: Step (in) - 2 - 3 - together (clap)   Meas. 5-6: Turn CCW (in place) - 2 - 3 - together (clap)
   Meas. 3-4: Step (out) - 2 - 3 - together (clap)   Meas. 7-8: Turn CW (in place) - 2 - 3 - together (clap)

☺ Teach verses B, C and D from a visual. Assign one group to each verse. Add movement.

PERFORMANCE - Rondo Form: A B A C A D A

A: All sing/move with orchestration
B, C, D: Each group speaks its verse with movement/motions. Encourage expressive speech.

EXTENSION - Rhythm Rondo

On the board, write four measures of rhythm in duple meter. Label this "A." Divide class into three groups (B, C, D). Provide two-beat rhythm cards. Groups create their own B, C, D sections, each eight beats long. Distribute unpitched percussion and have students practice their rhythms. Perform the rondo. (Everyone plays section A.)

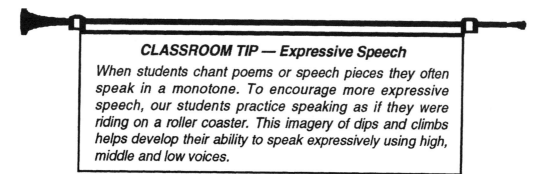

CLASSROOM TIP — Expressive Speech

When students chant poems or speech pieces they often speak in a monotone. To encourage more expressive speech, our students practice speaking as if they were riding on a roller coaster. This imagery of dips and climbs helps develop their ability to speak expressively using high, middle and low voices.

Mary Lee We Rolla Long

Traditional
arr. Dupont/Hiller

Variation 3 (pitches)

Mary Lee We Rolla Long

LEVEL: 4 - 5

FOCUS: Theme and variation

SKILLS: Recorder playing • Barred instrument playing • Note reading

PROCESS

☺ In pairs, teach the following movement. Maintain beat on a drum. Label this the "theme."

4/4															
pat	clap	pat	clap	walk	2	3	4	pat	clap	pat	clap	turn	2	3	4

legs own hands p's hands own hands (change places with partner)   (same as m. 1)   (in place)

☺ Have pairs vary the dance using different movements while maintaining the quarter note pulse. Next, have pairs vary the dance by altering the rhythms. Finally, have pairs perform the theme followed by each "variation." Maintain the beat on a drum.

☺ Present a visual of the *Mary Lee We Rolla Long* theme. Teach the melody as follows:
Sing note names as students finger pitches.
Play the melody as students finger pitches.
Students play the melody.

☺ Discuss ways a melody can be altered to create variations (change rhythm, add pitches, change meter, mode, dynamics).

☺ Present a visual of the *Mary Lee* variations. Play each variation and have students discuss how the theme has been altered.

☺ Divide the class into three groups, one for each variation. Teach each group its variation using the process in ☺3. Have a student play the corresponding bordun with each variation.

PERFORMANCE

All play the theme
Groups play their variations

EXTENSION 1 - Dance variations

Have students create partner dance variations (similar to those in ☺2) to accompany the recorder performance.

EXTENSION 2 - Composing variations

Present other simple melodies (*Twinkle, Twinkle* and *Row Your Boat,* etc.) and have students create their own variations using ideas found in this lesson.

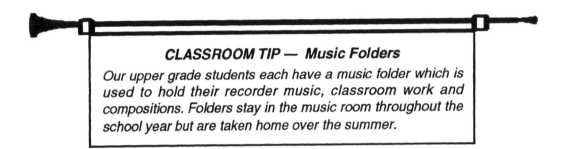

CLASSROOM TIP — Music Folders

Our upper grade students each have a music folder which is used to hold their recorder music, classroom work and compositions. Folders stay in the music room throughout the school year but are taken home over the summer.

Focus On Texture

Two, Four, Six, Eight

English Rhyme
arr. Dupont/Hiller

Two, Four, Six, Eight

FOCUS: Rhythm patterns over the beat

SKILLS: Steady beat • Instrument playing

PROCESS

❀   With students seated in a circle, teach the following chant, echoing by phrases. Have students pat the beat on their legs while speaking. Repeat until all names have been used.

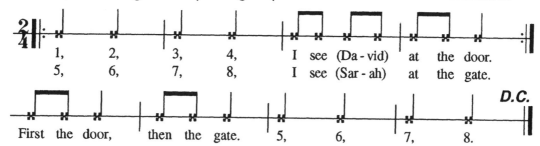

❀   Teach *Two, Four, Six, Eight* (section A), echoing by phrases. Have students pat the beat on their legs while singing.

❀   Divide the class into two groups. Have members of one group pat the beat on their legs while the other half sings and claps the rhythm of the text. Switch groups. Once students are secure, have them perform with body percussion only.

❀   Repeat above activity using drums for the beat and sticks for the rhythm of the text.

❀   Teach section B as follows: Divide class into four groups. Have one group maintain the steady beat on drums. Assign a different unpitched instrument to each of the three remaining groups as indicated in the score. Perform.

PERFORMANCE

Song (section A): Teacher plays a C-G chord bordun on a bass instrument.
Unpitched percussion (section B)
Song (section A)

EXTENSION - Improvisation

Assign one group of barred instruments (xylophones - metallophones - glockenspiels) set up in C Pentatonic, to each of the first three phrases of section B. After each four-beat phrase is sung have the corresponding barred instrument group improvise using the same rhythm. All instruments improvise the final phrase. Have several students play the C-G bordun on bass instruments.

> ### CLASSROOM TIP — Line 'em up!
> *In our kindergarten and first grade classes students line up by the colors they are wearing. We use a familiar song such as "The Farmer in the Dell" and change the words to "Line up if you're wearing green, line up if you're wearing green, hi-ho the dairy-o, line up if you're wearing green." Continue with other colors until all students are in line.*

One, Two, Three, Four, Five

Traditional
arr. Hiller

One, Two, Three, Four, Five

FOCUS: Three-part ostinati

SKILLS: Sixteenth notes • Rhythmic speech • Instrument playing

PROCESS

❀   Teach the following mouth sound piece, echoing by phrases. Divide the class into three groups, one for each part. Perform, layering in the parts.

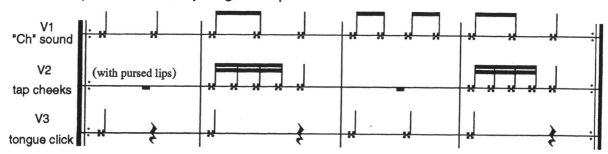

❀   Present a visual of *One, Two, Three, Four, Five*. Have students point out the similarities between both pieces. Teach V1, echoing by phrases.

❀   Once students are secure, teach V3. Divide class in half and perform both parts. Switch groups. If desired, further divide V1 into two parts for lines 3 and 4 to illustrate the question and answer.

❀   Teach V2. Perform the three-part ostinato, layering from the bottom up with groups taking turns on each part. Encourage expressive speech at all times.

❀   Transfer speech ostinati to body percussion: V3 = stamp, V2 = pat legs, V1 = clap. Perform first with speech, then with body percussion.

❀   Transfer body percussion to unpitched percussion: stamp = large percussion, pat legs = hand drums, clap = wood blocks/temple blocks.

PERFORMANCE

Speech: All speak V1
Speech ostinati: Layer in V3, V2, V1
Body percussion: Layer in V3, V2, V1
Unpitched percussion: Layer in V3, V2, V1

EXTENSION - Call and Response

Turn the piece into an orchestration—a conversation between xylophones and metallophones.

V3: Basses play a chord bordun on C and G.   V2: Bongo drums play.
V1: Meas. 1-2: Xylophones improvise in C Pentatonic using the rhythm of the phrase.
    Meas. 3-4: Metallophones improvise using the rhythm of the phrase.
    Continue in like manner to the end.

> ### *CLASSROOM TIP — Percussion Families*
> *We organize unpitched instruments in families for ease of access: metals, woods, skins, and large percussion. Instruments are kept in bins labeled by name and color-coded by family.*

Hear the Bells

Dupont/Hiller

Hear the Bells

FOCUS: Canon

SKILLS: 6/8 meter • Instrument playing • Level bordun

PROCESS

❁   Present the following visual. Teach as follows:

Speak rhythm syllables.
Speak/clap rhythm syllables.
Clap rhythms.

❁   Perform as a two-part canon, each group using a different body percussion. Once students are secure, perform as a three-part canon. Finally, perform as a four-part canon.

❁   Teach *Hear the Bells,* echoing by phrases. Encourage light, expressive vocal production.

❁   Prepare the orchestration with body percussion and text phrases, then transfer to instruments. Teach the BM and AM parts as a level bordun.

PERFORMANCE

Introduction: Layer in orchestration—BM, AM, SM (four meas.), unpitched percussion (four meas.)
Song in unison: Two times through
Two-part canon: Two times through
Optional interlude: (See below)
Three-part canon: Two times through
Four-part canon: Two times through
>   Each voice repeats the last two measures until all are singing in unison. Gradually fade out voices and orchestration.

EXTENSION - Interlude

Several advanced recorder players could learn the melody, then play the song in a two or three-part canon as an interlude during the performance.

To further experience the concept of canon, have students create movement to the song, changing after every two measures.

CLASSROOM TIP - Recorder positions

To avoid accidental "tooting" our students learn three recorder positions: (1) Rest position: the recorders hang from strings around students' necks. (2) Fingering position: students hold the mouthpiece under their chins and finger the notes without blowing. We also call this "the lollipop." (3) Playing position: students place recorders in their mouths, ready to play.

Focus On Harmony

Down Came a Lady

Traditional
arr. Dupont/Hiller

A

V — Down came a lady, down came two.
(2) three.
(3) four.

Down came a lady dressed in blue.
(2) dressed for the tea.
(3) out the door.

SG / AG

wood block — (Here she comes.)

BX / BM

B

1. La - dy, la - dy dressed in blue,
2. La - dy, la - dy dressed for tea,
3. La - dy, la - dy out the door,

why do you on - ly have one shoe?
when are you gon - na mar - ry me?
we can't sing this a - ny - more!

Down Came a Lady

FOCUS: Chord bordun

SKILLS: Steady beat • Instrument playing

PROCESS

X   To prepare students for playing the chord bordun, sing the song as students pat their legs to the half note pulse.

X   Teach the A section of *Down Came a Lady*, echoing by phrases.

X   Prepare the orchestration with body percussion and text phrases, then transfer to instruments.

X   Teach the B section, echoing by phrases.

X   <u>Movement</u>: Form one circle with three students in the center, one for each verse.
During the A section students join hands and walk the beat CW as they sing the song.
During the B section the three students take turns leading the group in a two-part body level pattern. (Ex. clap/pat legs or touch head/touch shoulders.)

PERFORMANCE

Song with orchestration (section A): Rotate students after each verse so more can have the chance to play the bordun accompaniment.
Speech with body level patterns (section B)

EXTENSION - Rhyme time

For additional practice in playing chord borduns, create new verses for the A section of the song that follow the rhyming pattern. Examples:
Down came a lady, down came five, down came a lady doing a jive.
Down came a lady, down came six, down came a lady picking up sticks.

CLASSROOM TIP — Photo Log

To quickly learn our students' names we take a photo of each group. We staple each photo to a piece of paper and write the students' names in the order they appear. This is placed in a binder with the class list and other pertinent information.

Springtime Magic

Dupont/Hiller

The sea - sons they go 'round and 'round, a ti - ny seed lies in the ground.

(Spring-time is here. Spring-time is here. Spring - time, spring-time is here.)

(Spring - time mag - ic.)

A lit - tle rain, a lit - tle sun, a lit - tle flow'r has just be - gun.

As spring-time breez-es gen - tly blow the lit - tle flow'r will grow and grow.

-28-

Springtime Magic

FOCUS: Crossover and level borduns

SKILLS: Instrument playing • Tone color improvisation • 6/8 meter

PROCESS

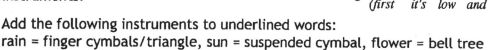

✗   Teach *Springtime Magic*, echoing by phrases.

✗   Prepare the crossover bordun by patting legs and and speaking the text in Exercise A. Transfer to bass instruments.

Exercise A
L   R   crossover L   R
(cross - ing o - ver, ne - ver un - der)

✗   Prepare the level bordun by patting legs/clapping hands and speaking the text in Exercise B. Transfer.

Exercise B
pat   clap
(first it's low and then it's high - er)

✗   Prepare the rest of the orchestration with body percussion and text phrases, then transfer to instruments.

✗   Add the following instruments to underlined words:
rain = finger cymbals/triangle, sun = suspended cymbal, flower = bell tree

✗   Present "Springtime Shower" visuals (below) and pair with the following instruments:
      sun = metallophones playing clusters   rain = glockenspiels
      wind = xylophones glissandi up and down   flower = bell tree

Point to visuals one or two at a time as students improvise. End with the flower.

PERFORMANCE

Song with orchestration   Springtime shower improvisation   Song with orchestration

EXTENSION - Springtime Flowers

Create a list of springtime flowers (crocus, daffodil, tulip, etc.). In small groups, have students create rhythmic phrases in 6/8 meter using flower names. These can be the flower names themselves or phrases that include a flower's description. Have students explore ways of integrating movement, body percussion, sound carpets, and instrumental sound color to accompany their "flower chant." These sections can be used with *Springtime Magic* to create a rondo.

CLASSROOM TIP - Mallet technique

We begin each year with a review of mallet technique. We remind students to hold the mallets in a relaxed manner, gently wrapping the fingers around them, elbows bent and out to the sides. We encourage players to bounce the mallet lightly off the center of the bars by practicing "walking" up and down the instrument with both mallets.

Viva la Musica

Viva la Musica

LEVEL: 4 - 5

FOCUS: I - IV - V chord progressions

SKILLS: Instrument/recorder playing • Speech ostinati • Composition

PROCESS

✗ Select a familiar song which uses a I-IV-V-I chord progression. (Ex. *When the Saints Go Marching In.*) Sing the song, playing only a I chord accompaniment on the piano. Have students raise their hands each time they hear the need for a chord change.

✗ Outline the I, IV, and V chords in the key of G on a musical staff. Identify the root, third and fifth of each chord with letter names.

✗ Display the *Viva la Musica* melody on a visual. Teach the song, echoing by phrases. Have students identify the first pitch in each measure and tell which chords contain these pitches. Determine through trial and error which chord progression best supports the song. Mark each chord above the melody.

✗ Once the chord roots are established, have students sing them on the downbeat of each measure (I-I-V-I, I-IV-V-I). Divide class in half. One group sings the chord progression as the other sings the song. Switch groups.

✗ Prepare the orchestration with body percussion and text phrases, then transfer to instruments.

✗ Divide the class into three groups. Teach the recorder interlude as follows:

Sing note names as students finger pitches.
Play the melody as students finger pitches.
Students play the melody.

✗ With students in three groups, teach the B section ostinati, echoing by phrases. Layer in each part from the bottom up. If desired, have students create accompanying movement.

-31-

PERFORMANCE

Song (section A) with orchestration
Recorder interlude with section A orchestration
Speech (section B) with unpitched percussion from section A
Song (section A) with orchestration
Recorder interlude with section A orchestration
Coda: All play meas. 5-6; all speak meas. 7-8 (no instruments); all play the final beat in meas. 8.

EXTENSION - Composition

Have students use the following worksheet to compose a melody which corresponds to these rhythms and chord progressions. Emphasize the need for downbeats to be a pitch in the chord. Encourage the use of passing tones between beats. Compositions can be played on recorders or barred instruments.

CLASSROOM TIP — Recorder Storage

To store and organize recorders we recycle large cans from our cafeteria and wrap them in contact paper. We label two cans for each class with the teacher's name and the letters "A-M" and "N-Z." Recorders are labeled with the students' names and stored in the can which corresponds with the first letter of their last names.

Instrument Glossary

SG - soprano glockenspiel
AG - alto glockenspiel

AX - alto xylophone
BX - bass xylophone

SM - soprano metallophone
AM - alto metallophone
BM - bass metallophone

SR - soprano recorder